KATE NICHOLSON

Paintings from the Artist's Studio

10 June – 1 July 2013

BELGRAVEST**i**VES

Modern & Contemporary Art

22 Fore Street · St Ives · Cornwall TR26 1HE

KATE NICHOLSON

Here is an inspired flow of words that could be applied directly to Kate Nicholson's paintings:

'… the rhythms, the variety, the weights, the aerial delight and certitude – as free as swallow's flight – no correction – no cloying sweetness …'

This was written by a potter about the 'linear brushwork' decorating an ancient Chinese stoneware jar. The potter was Bernard Leach. Kate knew him in St Ives, and surely listened intently to him. His eloquent words touch on the intuitive naturalness, the freshness, of her works no less than the pot they describe.

In the striking photograph by Pamela Chandler of Kate in her St Ives studio, beautiful pots gather on her large table. Pottery has been an emphatic inspiration for her, clearly, both in form and decoration. On the wall behind her is one of her own paintings. It is next to a white relief by Ben Nicholson, her father, and a hanging scroll or banner decorated with Eastern calligraphy. The meaning of this calligraphy would seem to lie in image and gesture, in movement and deftness quite as much as in language. In her abstract paintings Kate adopts and invents her own swift forms of 'calligraphy.' They speak for themselves in colour and brush-sweep. They seem to have leapt into existence with sudden energy and 'certitude' out of some kind of deep contemplation.

'*Nonchalance*' Leach also wrote, 'is a good word to describe the way the Koreans and other craftsmen of the East approach their work' He quickly added that nonchalance is by no means the same as sloppiness.

'… nonchalance and care are both present. It all depends on the spirit in which the work is done.'

Again he could be speaking of Kate's paintings. She, like Leach, tried to bring East and West together, exploring ways of balancing the West's mechanistic culture and personality-worship by an Eastern kind of craftsman's humility.

I first encountered her paintings years ago when Kate invited me down to St Ives. She persuasively suggested that as a very new writer-about-art something would be lacking if I had never been at least temporarily immersed in the St Ives atmosphere – clearly for her a centre of the art universe. She introduced me to several luminaries, including Bernard Leach. I could see that Kate held him in high regard. What was precisely said on that visit I do not really recall, but I do remember feeling his presence and his 'certitude' while sipping a delicate green tea. Here, I realised, were certain depths of thought and experience I had not been aware of before.

But today when looking at Kate's paintings, on very welcome display in Belgrave St Ives, past history is not what comes to mind. These paintings express nowness. They seem recent and new. The immediacy of a quick, vital swirl or curl, wave, ripple, flick, loop or upswing, is something sharply and swiftly in the present. These 'aerial delights' occur on the picture plane, or in some imagined space between the viewer's eyes and the canvas surface. There often are movements and colours interplaying and interweaving **behind** this prominent frontal happening. But all this movement has nothing to do with conventional linear perspective. Nor is it simply a descriptive foreground and background. It is – without being 'kinetic art' that actually moves – a liberated free flight.

In a letter to Kate, the painter Winifred Nicholson, her mother, talked about the 'gulf' of air between the very near (perhaps flowers on a windowsill) and very far (horizon or hill) that greatly engaged her attention. She suggested, however, that Kate might not see it that way. I believe that Kate didn't see it that way. Her work seems more a matter of near and nearer, rather than a contrast of very near and very far. As her work became more abstract, the energy and content of her paintings were less and less restricted by a recognizable subject. Their theme is increasingly the direct encounter of brush with canvas, of paint and gesture. 'Gesture' might be an ambiguous word here if it suggests some sort of theatricality, a performance act rather than an authentic experience. Kate was certainly aware of such apparently playful artists as Miro and Klee, and of 'action painting' or 'abstract expressionism.'

Her time as a student of Bath Academy of Art, taught by William Scott, would have made her fully aware of such things. She was particularly struck by the work of Mark Tobey, another artist bringing together Eastern and Western culture. But she found her own individual means of discovery.

There **is** playfulness in her work, a hop-skip-and-a-jump quality, but it is not showing off and it is not naïve. Nor does it carry sinister or surreal undertones. This sense of light-hearted play may have been inherited to some extent from Ben Nicholson, who on at least one recorded occasion joined in with the very young Kate and her older brother Jake, playing a game that involved rolling a ball around one of his reliefs. 'Fun' was a very allowable part of making art, however serious that art may be. The titles attached to her paintings have a poetry and humour that hint at this lightness of touch. These titles are not really frivolous or naïve, but have a kind of innocence: 'Spring Frolic' and 'Snatched in Short Eddies' in this exhibition join such earlier titles like 'Fancy Free' and 'Skip and a Twist' and 'Hay Diddle Diddle.'

'Liquid Sky' is another title that perfectly conveys one aspect of her work which connects the earlier, comparatively realistic paintings in this show with the later, more abstract ones. In these early landscapes, she is without question a wonderful and exciting painter of skies. She relishes the ever-moving changes of cloud and light. Her skies are not looming or ominous; they are filled with obvious delight as if she is saying 'Here is a realm where the very act of painting is set at liberty, where observation and imagination can mingle in a free cosmic dance.'

When her images have been most successful – like the marvellous 'Sun Dance' in this exhibition – Kate Nicholson has managed to invest her paintings with a remarkable balancing act. On one hand they seem evanescent and elusive. On the other they have bold strength and distinct permanence. The originality of her achievement deserves far greater recognition.

Christopher Andreae, April 2013

Lanercost and Mirage

Oil on board   76.5 x 78.5 cm

Signed and titled on backing board

Boothby View, Cumbria
Oil on paper   60 x 74 cm
Signed and titled on reverse

Untitled (Cumbrian Landscape)
Oil on board   61 x 122 cm
Provenance: The Artist's Studio

Quarry Beck, Cumbria
Oil on canvas board   46.5 x 71.5 cm
Signed and titled on reverse

Untitled (Cumbrian Landscape with Trees)
Oil on board 92 x 74 cm
Provenance: The Artist's Studio

Untitled (Hay Stack in Cumbrian Landscape)
Oil on canvas   81 x 100 cm
Provenance: The Artist's Studio

Grapes c1950
Oil on board   49.5 x 49.5 cm
Signed, titled and inscribed 'Monk's Park, Corsham, Wiltshire' on artist's label on reverse
Artist's handmade frame

Slumber 1962
Oil on paper laid on board   38 x 47.5 cm
Signed, titled and dated on reverse

Untitled (Still Life with Goblet and Bowl)
Oil on board   50.5 x 72 cm
Provenance: The Artist's Studio

Untitled (Goblet and Bowl)
Oil on board   50 x 61 cm
Provenance: The Artist's Studio

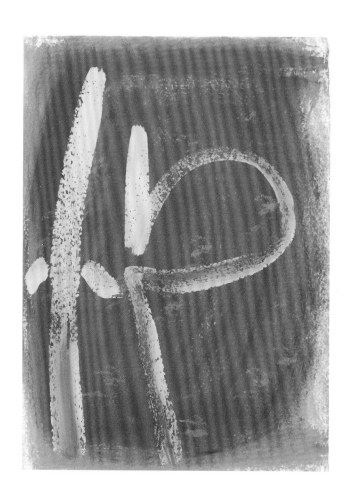

Untitled 1962
Oil on paper   39 x 28.5 cm
Provenance: The Artist's Studio

Untitled 1961
Oil on canvas   40.5 x 50.5 cm
Provenance: The Artist's Studio

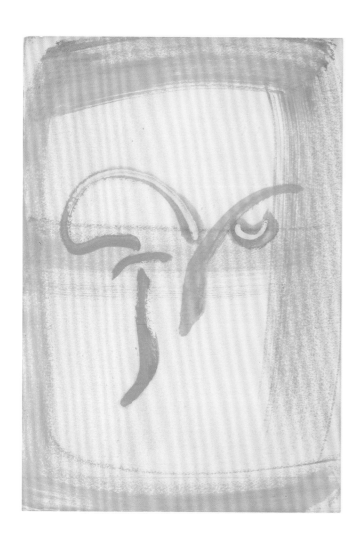

Untitled c.1962
Oil on paper   56.5 x 38.5 cm
Provenance: The Artist's Studio

Right: **Copper Smith** 1962
Oil on canvas   119.5 x 121.5 cm
Signed, titled and dated on stretcher bar
Exhibited: 'Kate Nicholson', Waddington Galleries, 1962, No.7

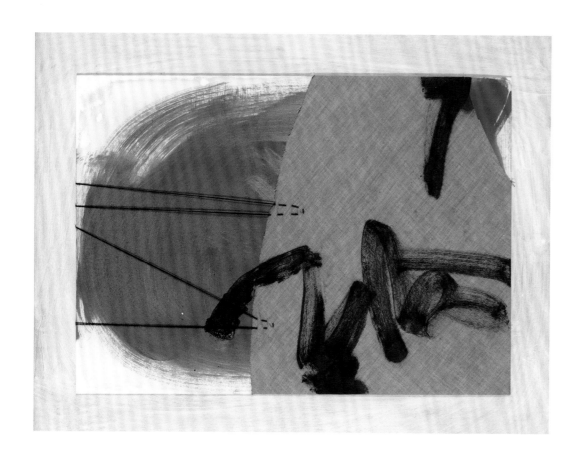

Snatched In Short Eddies 1961
Oil on paper with cloth collage on board   48.5 x 63 cm
Signed and dated on reverse
Exhibited: 'Kate Nicholson', Waddington Galleries, 1962, No.3

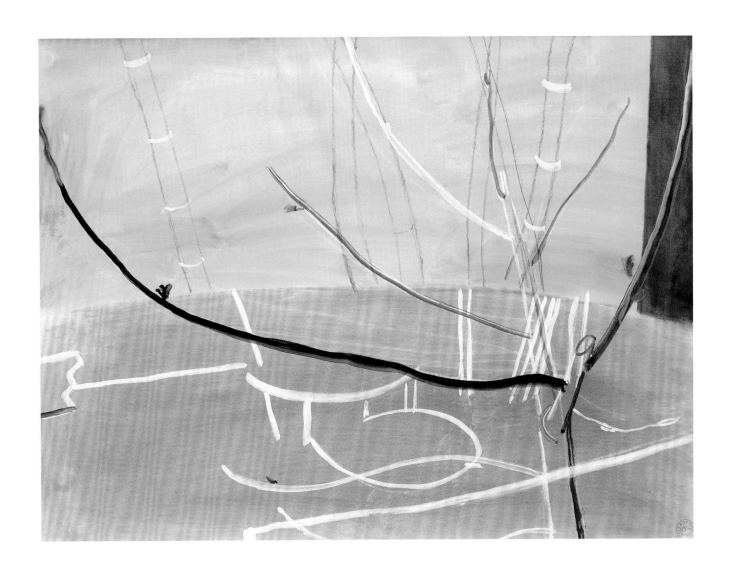

Growth of Green 1960
Gouache and charcoal on paper   70 x 92 cm
Signed, titled and dated on reverse
Exhibited: 'Six Young Painters', The Arts Council of
Great Britain, 1961, Cat No.15

Untitled
Oil on canvas laid on board   50 x 60 cm
Provenance: The Artist's Studio

The Corn is Growing 1962
Oil on paper laid on board   25 x 71 cm
Signed, titled and dated on reverse
Exhibited: 'Kate Nicholson', Waddington Galleries, 1962, No.43

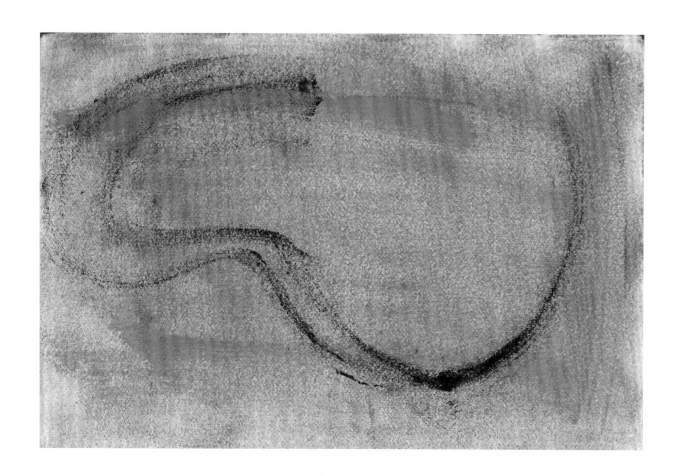

Troy 1963
Oil on paper laid on board   38 x 57 cm
Signed and dated on reverse

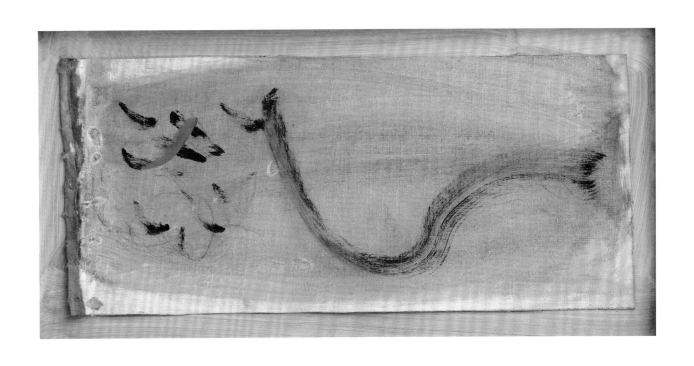

Tread of Passengers 1962

Oil on canvas laid on board   26 x 55 cm

Signed, titled and dated on reverse

Exhibited: 'Kate Nicholson', Waddington Galleries, 1962, No.5

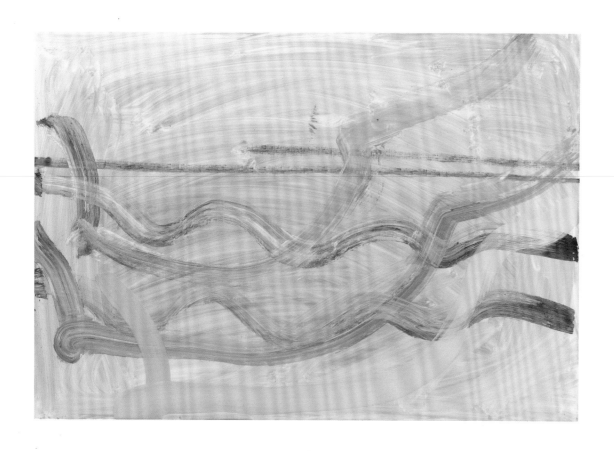

Sea Orchid 1966
Oil on canvas   60 x 87.5 cm
Signed, titled and dated on canvas overlap

Right: **Spring Cascade**
Oil on canvas   100 x 100 cm
Inscribed 'Ticino – Painted as staying with BN'
in the artist's hand on stretcher frame
Provenance: The Artist's Studio

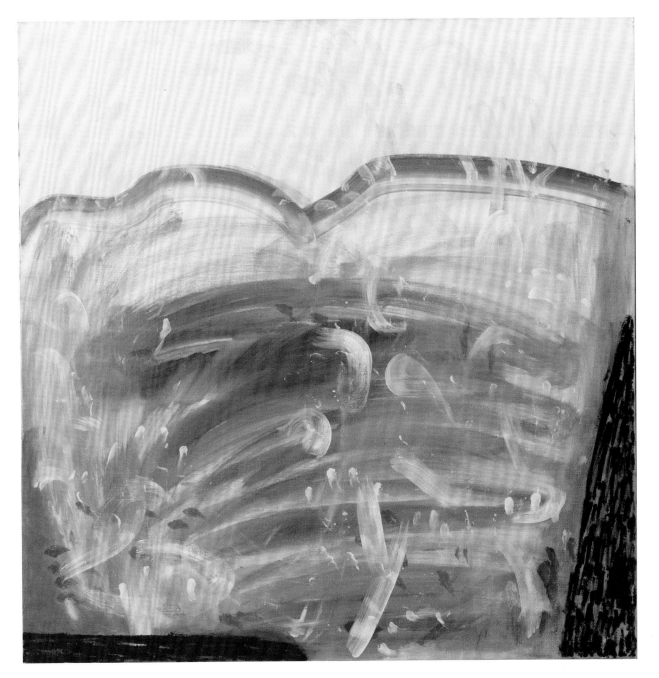

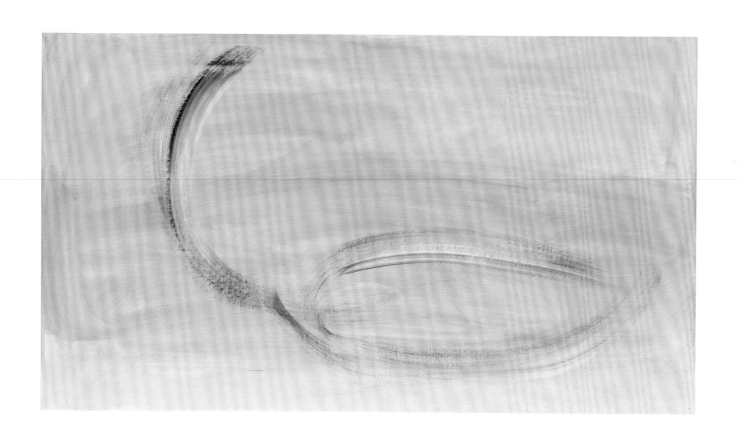

Lesbos
Oil on canvas   51 x 93.5 cm
Signed and titled on stretcher

The Throb of Silent Blue
Oil on canvas   60 x 89 cm
Signed and titled on stretcher frame
Exhibited: 'Peter Stuyvesant Northern Contemporaries'

Sea Salt
Mixed media   48 x 69 cm
Signed and titled on reverse

28

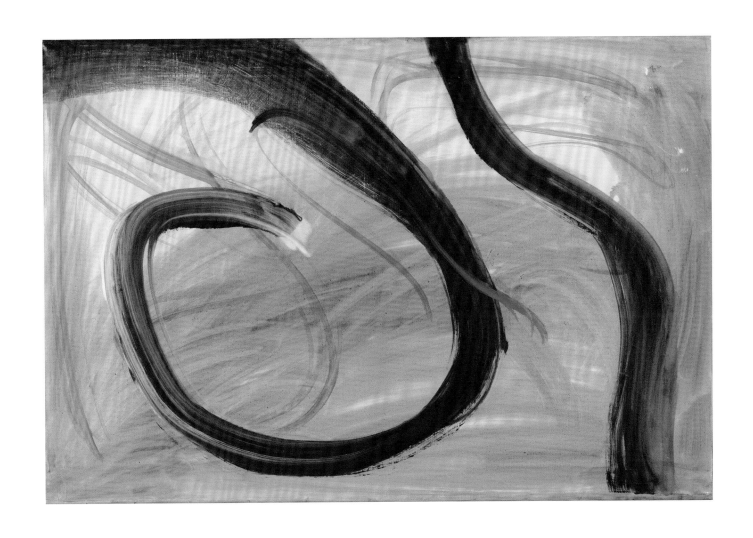

Ritual of Aversion 1966
Oil on canvas   59.5 x 89.5 cm
Provenance: The Artist's Studio

Message 1963
Oil on paper   37 x 48.5 cm
Signed, titled and dated on reverse
Exhibited: Penwith Society of Arts

Sun Dance 1980
Oil on paper   41.5 x 57 cm
Signed, titled and dated on reverse

Spring Frolic 1982
Oil on canvas   25 x 35 cm
Signed, titled and dated on reverse

Can Motion Be Expressed In Painting?

Written for an exhibition of Kate Nicholson's work, 1976.

If you look at the swell of the sea in a later Turner and the race of cloud across the sky of his canvas you will see that it **can** in a way.

The Chinese painters express it in a different way. They conceive a void which is utter stillness and through which symbols of cataracts, mountain peaks, and wandering sages meander.

Kate Nicholson expresses motion in yet another way. The entire theme of her paintings is interrelated flow. Space itself is in movement or waiting to move. In it, on the second plane, one sees slow movement but the movement nearest the onlooker is faster than lightning; it vanishes but returns into space. Its calligraphy does not travel out of the theme into a perspective of infinity; its dance is interwoven and interpenetrates the structure of the picture. The playground is the territory in front of the picture – between the picture canvas and the beholder – every bit as much as the territory behind the picture plane into which the magic casements open on to the fairy lands forlorn where Romantic art leads one.

Movement such as Kate Nicholson's must be taken into one's hand, must take one's hand to dance with it. It does not lead one away; it comes toward one. Of course, colour is the vehicle on which it comes. The chemistry of colour is the magic of the metamorphosis of line into movement. This crucible is at the spring of living forces, where chaos changes into the forces which give motive to the order of the universe. We tread on forces. Seek and feel these forces before they have crystallized into known objects with faces and personalities familiar to us.

Discard the superficial appearances that touch our eyes, discard the outer skins of objects we know and to whose language we are trained to reply.

Whence comes the wind?

Where are the roots of the ancient olive tree?

Where are the men of the bronze swords who were buried in the fiery red earth centuries ago?

Where are their thoughts?

Where are their dryads?

Is the love that fired them for fair Helen dead and gone?

And where, oh where, is the masterpiece of those unseen forces that will be painted tomorrow? Where is the flower-heart of the poem that will be sung next week?

In what star galaxy of the future lies the thought that these paintings evoke?

If one could measure the distance between the unborn child and the dissolving nebulae, then one could know the tension and the laughter into which Kate Nicholson dips her paintbrush, and know the answer to the question, 'Can a painting express motion?' The answer is that it cannot if the motion one thinks of is that of the motion picture, where phenomena appear and disappear into the oblivion of the stage screen. The motion that painting can express is to tell us where the impetus comes from, where it is going, and, not being in time but in eternity, one can travel backward as well as forward – not just winding the reel backward but knowing the source of all movement, its vibrations, its waves and its purposes, its destination – and follow these not with the physical eye, but with the one that tingles in the tips of one's fingers.

Winifred Nicholson

View of Porthgwidden Beach

KATE NICHOLSON

Born: Cumbria, 1929
Studied: Bath Academy of Art 1949-54
Moved to Cornwall: 1956

Selected solo exhibitions

2013   'Paintings from the Artist's Studio', Belgrave St Ives, Cornwall

1981   LYC Museum and Art Gallery, Cumbria

1975   Newcastle Municipal Gallery
        LYC Museum and Art Gallery, Cumbria

1974   'Kate Nicholson', Northern Arts Gallery, Newcastle

1970s   'Kate Nicholson, Paintings From a Journey in Morocco', Mignon Gallery, Bath,
        from 26th May - 24th June (listed in LYC catalogue 1981)

1970   'Kate Nicholson', Marjorie Parr Gallery, London

1969   'Paintings by Kate Nicholson', Border Art Gallery, Carlisle

1968   'Kate Nicholson: Greek Epigrams', Marjorie Parr Gallery, London

1966   'Kate Nicholson', Marjorie Parr Gallery, London

1962   'Kate Nicholson', Waddington Galleries, London

1959   'Kate Nicholson: Recent Paintings', Waddington Galleries, London

Selected group exhibitions

2012   'St Ives Exhibition', Belgrave St Ives, Cornwall

2011   'St Ives Exhibition', Belgrave St Ives, Cornwall

1998   'Modern British Art', Offer Waterman, London

1986   'Aspects of Modern British Art III', Austin Desmond Fine Art, London
        'Exhibition of Modern British Paintings', Michael Parkin Gallery, London

1985   'A Sense of Place…A Sense of Light, Cornwall', Parkin Gallery, London
        'St.Ives 1939-64; Twenty Five Years of Painting, Sculpture and Pottery',
        The Tate Gallery, London

1984   'Works by Kate, Winifred and Ben Nicholson', Wills Lane Gallery, St Ives

1983   'The Nicholsons', Crane Kalman, London

1981   'Kate Nicholson, Harvey Shields, Lawrence Upton', LYC Museum and Art
        Gallery, Cumbria

1979   Digby Gallery, Colchester

1970   'Helen Sutherland Collection', Arts Council touring exhibition, Hayward
        Gallery, London
        Laing Art Gallery, Newcastle upon Tyne
        Kettle's Yard, Cambridge
        National Museum of Wales, Cardiff
        Abbot Hall Art Gallery, Kendal

1967   'An Exhibition of Paintings by Roger Hilton, W. Barns Graham, Breon O'Casey,
        Kate Nicholson and Jeffrey Harris', Peterloo Gallery, Manchester
        34th Annual Exhibition Local Art, City Art Gallery, Carlisle

1966   33rd Annual Exhibition Local Art, City Art Gallery, Carlisle

1951-63 City Art Gallery, Carlisle

Public collections

Arts Council Collection
University of Cambridge
Fitzwilliam Museum, Cambridge
Kettles Yard Gallery, Cambridge
Pallant House Gallery, Chichster
Plymouth City Art Gallery
Cornwall Council Art Collection